Bloom
Thrive and Flourish After Trauma

Dr. Ivon L. Valerie

Sapiential Publishing

Bloom: Thrive and Flourish After Trauma
Copyright © 2025 by Apostle Dr. Ivon Valerie
All rights reserved.

Published by Sapiential Publishing House

No part of this publication may be reproduced, stored in a retrieval system, or transmitted in any form or by any means—electronic, mechanical, photocopying, recording, or otherwise—without the prior written permission of the author or publisher, except for brief quotations in critical reviews or articles.

Scripture quotations are taken from the King James Version (KJV), New International Version (NIV), New King James Version (NKJV), and English Standard Version (ESV), unless otherwise noted. Used by permission where applicable. All rights reserved.

This book is a work of non-fiction. Every effort has been made to ensure the accuracy of the information provided. The author and publisher disclaim any liability for any errors or omissions in the content of this book.

Cover Design: Sapiential Publishing House
Interior Design: Sapiential Publishing House

ISBN: 979-8-9928490-0-4

First Edition: 2025

Contents

Dedication	VII
Acknowledgements	IX
The Trauma Detox	XI
Introduction	XV
Proof of Healing	XIX
1. Rooting Into Your New Identity	1
2. Nurturing Supportive Relationships	9
3. Discovering Purpose and Direction	17
4. Building Resilience for Life's Challenges	25
5. Embracing Forgiveness and Letting Go	33
6. Cultivating Daily Joy	43
7. Stepping Into New Opportunities	57
8. Becoming A Source of Encouragement	69
9. Continuing to Bloom	81
Epilogue	93
What's Next	99

Dedication

To every heart that has survived the storm and still dares to bloom—this is for you.

To those who have been scarred, mended, and now stand ready to thrive—may your roots grow deeper, your branches stretch wider, and your life bears abundant fruit.

And to those still wondering if it's possible—you can, you will, and you must because blooming is your birthright.

Acknowledgements

Blooming is the final act in the story of survival, and I am humbled by the many hands that have helped me flourish along the way.

First and foremost, to my Creator—the ultimate Gardener of my life. You planted the seed, nurtured it through storms, and caused it to flourish in ways I never imagined.

To my wife, who has stood by me through seasons of drought and abundance—your love has been my living water. You are a crucial reason for my blooming. I love you.

To Sapiential Publishing House—thank you for nurturing these words and helping them reach those who need them most.

And to every reader—this book is more than pages and ink; it's a declaration that you are meant to thrive. May you rise, stretch, and bloom beyond what you thought possible.

THE TRAUMA DETOX

Throughout your healing journey, you've witnessed how trauma can infiltrate every corner of your life, staining your thoughts, your trust, and even the way you see yourself. **The Trauma Detox** series was designed to walk you through a thorough cleanse of that contamination—to confront its grip, methodically remove its residue, and emerge ready to embrace a fuller, freer existence.

- **Scarred** had you face the raw truths of your wounds, shining light on the hidden aches that shaped your daily struggles. It was about naming the pain so it wouldn't rule you in secrecy.

- **Mended** guided you through practical exercises and faith-based practices that, step by step, rebuilt your foundations. Each day, each boundary, each habit served to strengthen the soul that trauma once tried to crumble.

- **Bloom**, which you now hold, is the pinnacle of that detox process—no longer focusing solely on healing but on living beyond the scars. It calls you to flourish and channel your resilience into new experiences, relationships, and purpose.

You might ask, *"Why call it a detox?"* Because, like toxins, trauma residues can lodge deep in your emotions, body, and spirit. Each book in this trilogy addresses a dimension of that buildup: the acknowledgment of how deeply it runs (*Scarred*), the consistent purging of its effects (*Mended*), and finally, the flowering of a life set free from its reign (*Bloom*). This final book doesn't pretend your scars vanish entirely; instead, it shows how those scars can transition from sources of torment to marks of survival, fueling you with compassion for yourself and for a world full of wounded people.

Now that you've reached *Bloom*, you're ready for the wonder of living fully—rooted in the healing gleaned from earlier stages and blossoming in ways trauma tried to prevent. It's an invitation to maintain your healing and to stretch, serve, and shine. Because beyond your scars stand a destiny shaped by grace, and you are more than what tried to break you. You are, indeed, created to bloom.

Introduction

There comes a season in every journey where the fog of survival lifts, and you glimpse the vibrant colors of a life beyond mere getting by. You start to sense new possibilities, fresh purpose, and a level of freedom that trauma once seemed to steal. That's the heart of *Bloom*—an invitation to step past the threshold of basic healing and into a realm where your spirit thrives, your relationships grow rich, and your faith glows with forward-looking anticipation.

Maybe you've already done the deep work of naming your scars and establishing steady restoration routines. You've peeled away layers of shame and learned to guard your peace. Now, your soul doesn't just want to be well; it wants to flourish. You no longer see healing as a final destination but as a launching point for a life marked by joy, resilience, and divine purpose. This book, *Bloom*, walks you through that next horizon: living not as a survivor constrained by old wounds but as a person fully alive, rooted in renewed hope, and ready to share strength with others still wandering in the shadows.

We'll talk about discovering a fresh sense of meaning, walking daily in a freedom that no longer flinches at the echo of past trauma, and finding ways to pour out the abundance you've gained into the world around you. Think of it as a blossoming tree that has weathered storms. Its scars remain in the bark, but the canopy above is wide and green, offering shade and bearing fruit. You might still have moments where old memories tug at your thoughts, but now you face them from a position of growth, not defeat.

Yes, this is where you learn to dream again, to cultivate joy that overshadows your tears, and to stand confidently on a faith that has stood you in good stead through every valley. If *Scarred* taught you to name your pain and *Mended* helped you stabilize your heart, then *Bloom* leads you into a life of purpose, service, and genuine flourishing. Because, dear soul, you were never meant to remain in the hushed hush of trauma. You were fashioned to shine, blossom, and become a testimony that growth can spring from even the harshest soil.

So, welcome to the next chapter of your healing story. May this book remind you how strong your roots are and how vast your branches can spread when nurtured by love, faith, and grace. Let's step together into the fullness of life that beckons you—beyond survival, beyond mere recovery—to a place where your spirit blooms in radiant color. Let's begin.

Proof of Healing

Jasmine's Story

Trauma makes you believe survival is the best you can hope for.

For years, I lived stuck in survival mode—hyper-aware, constantly bracing for the next hit, the next betrayal, the next loss. Thriving? Flourishing? That was for people who hadn't lived through what I had.

When I crossed paths with Apostle Dr. Ivon Valerie, I was burned out on "healing." Therapy helped me survive, but I wanted to live.

He told me something that changed everything: "You weren't created to live in survival mode forever. Healing isn't the end of the story—it's the soil where growth begins."

We didn't focus on what I'd lost. We focused on what was still possible.

Through his guidance, I stopped waiting for life to happen and started creating it. I rediscovered my passions, stepped into leadership roles I never thought I could handle, and built healthy, life-giving relationships.

But the most significant shift? I stopped seeing myself as a victim of my past and started seeing myself as the author of my future.

Blooming wasn't about erasing my scars—it was about letting them fuel my growth.

Chapter 1

Rooting Into Your New Identity

Close your eyes momentarily and imagine a seed planted deep in the soil. Once battered by storms, it finds nourishment in fresh, life-giving earth. The seed sends out roots, inch by inch, searching for stability and moisture. Over time, it pushes upward, breaking through the surface to reveal a tender sprout, poised to become something far greater than its humble beginnings. That's the picture of you stepping into *Bloom*: you're no longer defined by trauma's storms; you're discovering a deeper, richer identity, digging roots into truth, and reaching toward the light that once felt unreachable.

Trauma can cling to you like a sticky name tag, labeling you in ways that distort your view of yourself. It might have stamped you as "damaged," "unworthy," or "unlovable." In the darkest chapters, you might have believed those labels were facts. But now, through your healing journey, you realize that none of those old tags have a rightful place in your identity. They were forced upon you by pain, the harsh voices of the past, or your wounded self-perception.

Embracing a new identity begins by peeling off those false labels. Think of it as removing an old, grimy sticker from a precious piece of furniture. It might resist at first and leave a residue behind, but with patience and care, the original surface emerges clean and unblemished. In the same way, each day, you reaffirm the truths you uncovered in healing: *I am resilient, I am worthy, and I am not my scars.* Over time, that residue of shame and fear lifts, unveiling the essence of who you truly are—a soul fashioned for growth and flourishing.

Sometimes, it takes stepping back to see how far you've come. You might recall early in your recovery when trust felt impossible or every trigger left you trembling. Now, though challenges remain, you react with more grace, more faith, and more confidence. These changes aren't accidents; they're the fruit of the seeds you've planted—seeds of self-compassion, prayerful habits, and daily acts of courage. As you recognize this transformation, you reinforce a stronger identity: *I am someone who can learn, adapt, and thrive.*

Let your healing experiences form the lens through which you view yourself today. Instead of fixating on a leftover scar, remember the determination to move from *Scarred* to *Mended*. That journey has rewritten the narrative in your mind, proving that trauma doesn't get the final word. You do. Your new identity includes facets like empathy, wisdom, and resilience that can only come from enduring trials and emerging more whole on the other side.

The world tries to mold our identities in countless ways—through social expectations, family pressures, or cultural definitions of success. But when you've tasted the pain that trauma inflicts, you realize those external opinions often fall short of giving you absolute security. True identity flourishes when anchored in something unwavering, like God's love, which calls you by name and recognizes you as His cherished creation.

Anchoring yourself in God's truth means repeatedly telling your heart: *I am not defined by what happened to me but by the One who holds me.* Whether it's a Scripture verse that resonates with your journey—perhaps *"I am fearfully and wonderfully made"*—or a simple whispered prayer of belonging, each time you recite that truth, your roots grow a bit deeper. Over time, you'll notice your self-image aligning more with God's perspective than with the false narratives trauma tried to enforce.

Some survivors battle an internal bully—a voice that critiques every step, belittles every achievement, and questions every hope. Recognizing and confronting that bully is key to rooting into your new identity. You've put in real work—admitting your scars, caring for your mind and body, opening yourself to the possibility of joy again. That deserves a baseline respect for who you are becoming. Imagine you see a friend making strides in their growth; you'd cheer them on, wouldn't you? Offer yourself that same encouragement. Treat yourself with the kindness you've long given to others.

Healthy self-respect doesn't imply arrogance or narcissism. Instead, it means valuing the person God fashioned, acknowledging the challenging roads you've navigated, and permitting yourself to walk with your head a little higher because you survived a season designed to break you. Let the knowledge of your healing power fill you with a steady confidence that you can face whatever tomorrow brings.

As your identity shifts, your actions often follow suit. You might find yourself drawn to new activities or relationships that mirror the freedom you're stepping into. Embrace them. Seek friendships that recognize your worth, not those who dismiss your boundaries or undermine your growth. If an old environment constantly pulls you back into negativity or fear, consider whether to limit your exposure or find new spaces that encourage your continued blooming.

This also means leaving behind habits that no longer serve you. Coping mechanisms you needed when you felt cornered by trauma—like avoidance, self-isolation, or numbing behaviors—might no longer fit your present self. Replacing them with healthier outlets—creative pursuits, spiritual disciplines, or communal gatherings—reinforces that you're living from a place of hope rather than desperation.

As you root into this renewed identity, you might sense an urge to share parts of your journey with others—whether through mentorship, testimonies, or casual conversations where you speak life into someone battling a similar darkness. That's the beauty of healing: it often overflows, watering souls still parched by trauma. The moment you realize your scars can help another person see the path is when your identity takes on an added dimension: *I'm not just a survivor; I'm also an encourager, a living proof that renewal is possible.*

Remember, you choose how, when, and with whom you share your story. There's no rush. But if an opportunity arises where your transparency might spark someone's hope, trust the gentle nudge of your spirit. Vulnerability in the proper context can be a powerful ministry, turning your once-broken places into a bridge for another's healing.

At this stage, you're no longer clinging to survival but daring to bloom. Let each day be an opportunity to embrace the identity you've cultivated—somebody shaped by wounds but defined by resilience, loved by God, and capable of ongoing transformation. Like a plant that has taken root in nourishing soil, watch your life unfold in ways you never thought possible. Where once you felt restricted by fear, you now see open fields of possibility.

Bloom is the journey of walking confidently in who you've become. It's about letting your roots sink deeper into faith, your petals open wider to love, and your influence reaches further to uplift. There might still be storms, but now you have a foundation that steadies you. Your identity isn't tied to the chaos that happened to you; it's grounded in the redemptive power carrying you beyond those memories.

So take heart, beloved soul. You're not just "not scarred" anymore; you're blooming—vibrant, wholehearted, and ready to live from the core of a new identity that trauma can't define or destroy. Let each sunrise remind you of how far you've come, and each sunset fills you with gratitude for the promise of a tomorrow that glows with even more light. There is abundant life ahead, and you are exactly the person, newly rooted, ready to embrace it fully.

Reflection Questions

1. What labels has trauma placed on you that no longer serve your growth?

2. How has your past shaped your view of yourself, and how is God redefining that view?

3. What is one lie you believed about yourself that you now know isn't true?

4. What new identity are you stepping into as you heal?

5. How can you root yourself deeper in God's truth about who you are?

CHAPTER 2

Nurturing Supportive Relationships

Y ou're in a warm, sunlit room, sharing laughter and honest conversation with someone who genuinely cares about you: no pretense or hidden agenda—just a safe space for your heart, to be honest. For many who've survived trauma, that sort of genuine connection can feel about as rare as a blooming rose in the desert. You might have felt alone for so long that trusting another person's compassion seems risky. Yet God wired us to thrive in the company of others, to bear one another's burdens, and to celebrate victories side by side.

A life that blossoms—from survival to true flourishing—needs relationships that uplift rather than drain, that foster authenticity rather than demand performance. These relationships become the backdrop for your continued growth, reminding you that isolation isn't your natural habitat. Over time, you'll discover that intentionally nurturing these connections can heal scars you once believed no one else could understand.

It's natural to be cautious if past friendships or family ties have disappointed you. You might hesitate to open up again, bracing for disappointment or betrayal. However, consider how seeds only take root in the soil by risking the dark unknown beneath the surface. In that same spirit, forging supportive bonds often involves risking vulnerability—allowing someone a glimpse into your world, even if you can't control how they'll respond.

But, despite the vulnerability, there's immense reward. A friend who truly listens when you share your anxieties offers more than comfort; they validate your feelings and affirm your worth. A supportive pastor or mentor who prays with you during a tough week doesn't just reduce your loneliness; they remind you that God's love can be channeled through the empathy of others. Over time, these moments add up, fueling your belief that trust is not a lost cause.

In this blooming season, consider who belongs in your inner circle. It might be one or two close friends, a small group from church, or a blend of mentors and peers who understand your journey. You don't need a huge crowd; the most nurturing relationships often stem from intimate connections where hearts meet in honesty.

Take stock of current relationships. Which ones bring a sense of calm or hope when you talk, and which leave you tense or unseen? Which ones celebrate your progress rather than undermining it? By identifying those who consistently build you up, you craft a circle of people who can shoulder some weight when life feels heavy. Be mindful, though: supportive relationships flourish best on mutual respect. As they give, you also learn to give back—through listening, prayer, and encouragement—making the bond richer for both parties.

Nurturing supportive relationships calls for a balance between honesty and discretion. There's no need to overshare your entire trauma history with every acquaintance. But you can let someone trustworthy see past the mask you wear daily. That initial disclosure might be small—like admitting you're having a tough day or that crowds sometimes trigger your anxiety. If they receive your words compassionately, you can share more next time, gradually weaving a deeper sense of trust.

Don't be surprised if it takes time to build these connections. Just as it took time to mend your internal wounds, relationships also take time to reach a depth where vulnerability feels safe. Please don't rush the process; let it unfold. And if a conversation ever leads to hurt or misunderstanding, treat it as an invitation to clarify boundaries or communicate more clearly. Real friendships can handle honest moments without collapsing in judgment.

Genuine support goes both ways. As you find safe people who listen to your story, consider how you can speak life into theirs. Ask about their struggles, cheer on their victories, and be present when they're navigating their storms. Love that flows in a single direction soon stagnates, but love that's reciprocal transforms a mere friendship into a life-giving bond. This reciprocity doesn't deny that you're healing; it recognizes you have the grace and strength to share while healing.

In a faith context, you can build these supportive relationships through small groups, prayer partners, or shared service projects. A unique unity arises when you labor alongside someone—be it volunteering in a soup kitchen or organizing a fellowship event. You learn each other's personalities, weaknesses, and strengths, forging bonds beyond weekly pleasantries.

At the core of every meaningful relationship stands a shared understanding, a common ground. For many, faith supplies that foundation. When two people believe that God is intimately involved in healing hearts, it changes how they approach each other's scars. Instead of offering shallow sympathy, they pray over you with expectancy. Instead of cold advice, they provide a listening ear fueled by the Spirit's compassion.

This spiritual anchor guards against the superficial. You learn that you can kneel with a friend, tears in your eyes, and sense God's presence in their comforting hand on your shoulder. You can confess your fear of slipping backward, and they can gently remind you that God's grace has carried you this far and won't abandon you now. Over time, such moments accumulate into a sense of belonging that trauma once told you was impossible.

For some, the most complex relationships to navigate are within the family. Old patterns, decades of unresolved tension, or differences in faith or personality can make healing feel like an uphill climb. But even here, nurturing supportive ties is not out of reach. You could start by setting firmer boundaries that protect you from toxic behaviors. Or, you schedule intentional one-on-one time with a sibling or parent who genuinely respects your journey. If healthy reconciliation proves too difficult with certain relatives, you might limit interactions, finding your "family" in people who show you the acceptance and kindness your blood relatives cannot.

In all family dynamics, patience is essential. They might still see the "old" you who was silent or emotionally guarded, not realizing how much you've grown. Gently show them you're different now—asserting boundaries, speaking honestly, forgiving but not allowing mistreatment. This redefines the relationship if they're willing or clarifies it if they're not. Either outcome can still be part of your ongoing transformation.

As you step further into your identity as someone surviving and thriving, relationships become a greenhouse for your continued bloom. They offer the sunlight of understanding and the water of encouragement. You share your grace and empathy, helping others bloom beside you. Watching yourself and your circle of friends or family grow in resilience and faith is profound fulfillment.

Yes, vulnerability remains a risk. Yes, trust can be broken at times. But the alternative—living behind walls of solitude—blocks the connection God intended for your wholeness. So dare to engage. Dare to let a friend see your tears or celebrate your breakthroughs. Dare to ask for prayer when life feels stormy and return that blessing when someone else's clouds roll in. As you do, you'll find that healing flourishes best in community, a network of souls knit together by divine love.

In this new season, you are ready to nurture supportive relationships that amplify the healing you fought to claim. May your courage inspire others, and may you find a reflection of the Father's heart in their company. This heart never intended you to walk alone, but in fellowship that fosters hope, accountability, and a deeper sense of belonging. Let your connections be the soil that strengthens your roots, ensuring that your bloom is not a fragile moment but an enduring testament to the power of companionship on this journey of continued growth.

Reflection Questions

1. What relationships in your life have helped you heal, and what relationships have held you back?

2. Have past hurts made it difficult for you to trust others? How can you begin opening your heart again?

3. Who in your life encourages your growth and speaks life into you? How can you invest more in those connections?

4. What boundaries do you need to set to protect your peace and well-being?

5. How can you be more intentional in building relationships that nurture your healing and joy?

Chapter 3

Discovering Purpose and Direction

A fter speaking at a conference, I met Jason, who asked me, "Where do I go from here?" Perplexed, I asked him to explain his question. "I feel like I'm standing at a crossroads, the memories of my past wounds fading behind me, and in front of me an open horizon that begs the question: *Where do I go from here?*" he elaborated. *Jason's question sincerely touched me. I could see in his eyes that all he wanted was a clear direction.* After the storms of trauma, it's tempting to live each day simply grateful you survived. Yet our human spirits yearn for more than mere survival; they long to find meaning—a sense of calling that resonates in the deepest chambers of our hearts. In this new blooming season, discovering your purpose and direction becomes integral to your ongoing transformation.

When trauma was fresh, your energy likely went into coping, shielding yourself from further harm, or rebuilding essential trust. But now, as you've journeyed through healing, your perspective can expand. Instead of fixating on scars, you sense a stirring—a desire to take the lessons you've learned and the empathy you've gained and channel them into something beyond yourself. That stirring, that gentle nudge, often comes from God's Spirit, prompting you to walk forward with greater clarity about how you're meant to impact the world around you.

Purpose doesn't always shout in neon lights or dramatic visions. Sometimes, it's found in the quiet resonance of your heart when you're doing a small act of kindness or using a skill that brings you joy. You pause and think, *"This feels right. I could do this even on a hard day."*

That alignment is a clue to the path unfolding beneath your feet—*a path that honors your past and transforms it into a story of redemption.*

We often see healing as the end goal—getting to a place where triggers are less severe, boundaries are well-established, and emotions feel more balanced. But healing can also serve as a springboard into your next chapter. Traumatic experiences, when honestly faced and tenderly mended, can deepen your compassion, refine your gifts, and broaden your understanding of how we all struggle. These qualities can shape a sense of calling far more significant than if you'd never encountered adversity.

Think of biblical figures who endured hardship—Joseph, Ruth, and even Paul. Their hardships didn't disqualify them; they equipped them. Similarly, your journey from *Scarred* to *Mended* can fuel a purpose grounded in empathy. Maybe you find yourself drawn to mentoring young people who face the same insecurities you once battled, or you develop a passion for advocating for mental health in your community. The pain of yesterday becomes the compass for your tomorrow, guiding you toward a purpose that benefits you and lights a path for others.

As you contemplate your direction, notice the quiet sparks that ignite your enthusiasm. When you hear about a specific cause, does something in you leap? Do you feel a tug to write, teach, counsel, create art, build a business that uplifts people, or show love in practical ways? These tiny flickers can point to where your unique calling lies. Prayer and reflection help clarify these signals. *"Lord, show me what breaks Your heart that should also break mine"* can be a powerful question, aligning your gifts with God's compassion.

If you're unsure, experiment. Volunteer for a local outreach. Try a class or workshop in an area that intrigues you. You might discover your passion lies in organizing events that unite people or quietly offering one-on-one support to someone who feels alone. As you take these exploratory steps, pay attention to where your heart feels at peace, where your mind feels energized, and where you sense the Spirit nodding approval.

It's not uncommon to second-guess your ability to step into a purposeful life. Fear might whisper, *"I'm too wounded, too flawed, too behind."* But remember, every chapter of healing has chipped away at such lies. If you overcome the shadows of trauma, you can certainly face the voices of self-doubt. Remind yourself of the growth you've experienced—how you learned to ground anxious thoughts, speak your truth, and form supportive relationships. Those same muscles of resilience will help you navigate new challenges.

Sometimes, practical obstacles arise—financial strains, lack of time, or familial responsibilities. Embracing purpose doesn't necessarily mean drastic changes overnight. It can be integrated into your current context with creativity. Maybe you volunteer a few hours a month rather than launching into a full-time endeavor. Or you can find ways to weave your passion into your existing commitments. The key is to keep your heart open, trusting that if God has placed a specific burden on your soul, He'll also provide a path forward if you're willing to take it one step at a time.

At each turn, invite God into the decision-making process. Scriptures say, "In all your ways acknowledge Him, and He will direct your paths." This isn't about waiting for a thunderous revelation; it's about cultivating a daily awareness of His presence in your plans. You might jot down your ideas, pray over them, and ask for doors to open if they align with His will or close if they don't. Guidance often flows through subtle confirmations—a timely conversation, a coincidence that feels too purposeful to be random, or an inner peace that persists despite external uncertainties.

Let your faith community or trusted mentors pray with you about these stirrings of purpose. Two or three faithful voices speaking wisdom can provide the clarity you might not see on your own. If you sense fear rising, be honest about it. Fear doesn't disqualify you; it simply means you're stepping into territory that matters. Courage is fear that has said its prayers and decided to keep going anyway.

As you discover how your gifts and experiences fit together, you'll likely realize your purpose isn't just about self-fulfillment; it's also about service. Even a flower that blooms in solitude offers nectar to bees, contributes oxygen, or brings joy to those who pass by. In the same way, your blossoming can naturally overflow into acts of kindness or initiatives that uplift others. This synergy is beautiful: as you pour out, you also find yourself replenished by the satisfaction of a life lived in alignment with your higher calling.

Service doesn't have to be grandiose. A few heartfelt conversations with someone who feels unseen can have ripple effects you never anticipate. A small group you lead, or an event you help organize can ignite hope in hearts that desperately need it. Let your personal healing story become a beacon of possibility for those still slogging through the darkness. The essence of sharing purpose is transforming your scars into signposts pointing others to the same hope that carried you.

Purpose and direction aren't static; they can evolve as you grow. You might start off volunteering in one area and discover a spark for something entirely different. Be flexible. A life that blooms, adapts, learns, and follows where God's Spirit leads. Sometimes, you'll face setbacks—new challenges or unexpected detours. But each test, handled with faith, can deepen your sense of calling rather than diminish it.

Remember, *Bloom* is about living fully beyond the wounds of the past. Finding and following your purpose is a cornerstone of that fullness, a declaration that you refuse to be defined solely by what you overcame. Instead, you allow the lessons, compassion, and renewed strength you've gained to guide you into a future that transcends trauma. Your direction may not look like anyone else's, and that's okay. God has a unique design for every blossoming soul.

So lift your eyes to the horizon. If you feel a stirring to teach, encourage, create, counsel, or lead, lean into it prayerfully. Let your scars become stepping stones to a purpose bigger than your pain. In that vision lies the promise that once marked by brokenness, your story can unfold into a testimony of hope for a world that desperately needs living examples of how grace and determination can turn ashes into beauty. That's the kind of life that genuinely blooms.

Reflection Questions

1. When you think about your life's purpose, what desires stir in your heart?

2. How has your trauma shaped your ability to help others?

3. What passions or talents have been buried under your pain that you're ready to revive?

4. Where do you sense God calling you to make an impact?

5. What steps can you take today to walk toward a more purposeful life?

CHAPTER 4

Building Resilience for Life's Challenges

Have you ever watched an oak tree sway in a fierce windstorm? I had the pleasure of watching a video of the mighty oak tree swaying to the force of the wind. Its leaves whip about, and branches shudder under the onslaught, yet the trunk holds firm, roots gripping the earth as though refusing to yield. That's resilience: not an absence of struggle but a determined capacity to bend without breaking, to endure trials, and to emerge stronger. In this blooming phase of your healing journey, you must cultivate a similar inner fortitude that helps you meet life's challenges head-on, secure in faith and self-awareness.

Life rarely unfolds according to our neatest plans. Even after significant healing, new crises or setbacks can appear: a sudden financial strain, a job loss, or friction in a key relationship. Trauma survivors, especially, might interpret these events as proof they'll never be free of turmoil. But resilience doesn't deny difficulties; it insists that adversity won't have the last word. When you foster resilience, you anchor yourself in the unshakable truth that you've faced storms before, and by grace, you can do it again.

Sometimes, you'll see the storm forming on the horizon. Other times, it'll roar in without warning. Either way, resilience helps you pivot from panic to problem-solving, from despair to a measured response. It's not about feigning positivity. Instead, it's about quietly telling yourself, *"I have resources, I have faith, and I have come through darkness before. This moment, too, will pass."*

Look at the coping strategies you've learned—breathing exercises, grounding techniques, boundary-setting, journaling, or prayerful reflection. These are your toolkit, not just for past traumas but for any fresh challenge that emerges. Resilience grows every time you use these tools effectively in the face of new problems. Each time you say, "Okay, let me pause and breathe before reacting," or "I'll pray about this fear rather than letting it eat me alive," you reinforce neural pathways that favor calm over chaos.

You might be surprised how second nature these methods become. A heated argument arises, and you instinctively practice a quick body scan to see if you're clenching your fists or holding your breath. A wave of anxiety crashes in, and you find yourself whispering, *"Lord, I trust You,"* before despair can grip your heart. Remember the first time you tried these techniques? They may have felt awkward, but now they're part of your daily arsenal—building a habit of resilience one reaction at a time.

When life's challenges surge, resilience often comes down to the strength of your community. We're not meant to handle every burden alone. Maybe you have a friend you can text for an encouraging scripture or a family member who listens without judgment. Even online faith groups or in-person small circles at church can become lifelines, reminding you that you're not isolated in your battles. They help you step outside your head, gather fresh perspectives, and soak up prayers that sustain your endurance.

Fostering such relationships beforehand is crucial. In times of relative calm, nurture your support system by checking in, showing empathy for others, and allowing them to do the same for you. Then, when an unforeseen challenge arrives, you already have connections of trust to lean on. Resilience thrives in communal warmth. Just as a lone coal quickly dies out, but embers glow longer when clustered together, your spirit remains fortified by caring allies.

Sometimes, a new wave of adversity can trigger feelings of shame—*"I should've been better prepared,"* or "I should be stronger by now."* Shame is a crafty foe, especially for those who've walked through trauma, because it tries to convince you that setbacks define you. Yet resilience recognizes that stumbling or feeling overwhelmed doesn't negate your growth. It's simply another chapter where your character is tested and refined.

Replace shame with self-compassion. If you lose your temper or find yourself crying unexpectedly, forgive yourself for the slip. Then, use it as a cue to gently re-engage your faith and coping strategies. Remind yourself, *"I'm allowed to be human; I'm allowed to feel. This does not erase my progress—it's a chance to apply what I've learned."* That posture helps you bounce back faster, reaffirming that healing is a lifelong journey, not a one-and-done event.

In a deeper sense, resilience is anchored not just in psychological tools but in a grounded faith that proclaims, *"God is with me, no matter how heavy this storm feels."* As you continue blooming, let this assurance be your foundation. Start your day by saying, *"I trust Your presence today, Lord, and I know You'll guide me in every unexpected challenge."* Then, when trials arise, you're already leaning on a mindset of trust rather than scrambling for it in panic.

This faith-forward approach transforms each hardship into an opportunity to deepen your connection with God. Instead of viewing trouble as evidence you're cursed or unworthy of blessings, you see it as a scenario where God's sustaining grace will become even more evident. You can talk to Him plainly: "Lord, I'm scared, but I believe You stand with me. Help me see how I can grow through this crisis." Resilience isn't just a psychological trait; it's a spiritual posture shaped by encounters with a faithful God who never abandons you.

Resilience isn't about not trembling; it's about trembling and choosing to move forward anyway. Each time you do, you discover a fresh layer of strength you didn't know you had. And that kind of self-discovery feeds into the broader picture of your blooming season. Suddenly, you're no longer running from problems; you're navigating them with a quiet sureness rooted in all you've learned and the One you trust.

And yes, some challenges might still knock you down. But now, the floor doesn't feel so final. You've built the reflex to stand up, reach for a friend's hand, whisper a prayer for courage, and step again. This is the rhythm of resilience: stumble, learn, adapt, and rise. Over time, you'll look back and marvel at how the storms that once nearly destroyed you became proving grounds for the unwavering spirit that now dwells in your heart.

In the grand design of your healing, resilience is the thread weaving through every chapter. It says to your fears, *"I see you, but you won't rule me,"* and to your faith, *"I trust that strength and grace will meet me in every valley."* Nurture that thread, keep it strong, and watch how your life expands with confidence that future storms can't steal. You stand, arms open, blossoming in the knowledge that what tried to bend you can no longer break you. That is resilience, and it's your living testimony to the power of hope in a once-devastated soul.

Reflection Questions

1. What has been your first reaction to setbacks in the past? How has that changed as you've healed?

2. How can you develop a mindset that faces trials with faith rather than fear?

3. What are the spiritual and practical tools you rely on to stay strong in difficult times?

4. How can you see past struggles as preparation for the future rather than punishment for the past?

5. What scripture or truth anchors you when life's storms feel overwhelming?

Chapter 5

Embracing Forgiveness and Letting Go

I'm about to ask you to do something that might be uncomfortable, but trust me, you can do it. I want you to remember the last time you felt the weight of an old hurt pressing heavily on your heart. Perhaps it was a quiet ache at dawn or a sudden rush of anger when a memory caught you off guard. Trauma has a way of leaving these invisible shackles around your soul—shackles that tug at your joy, your hope, and even your faith. Forgiveness and letting go might seem impossible, especially when your wounds still feel raw. But, in this phase of blooming, learning to release the burdens of resentment becomes the very thing that propels you toward a future not ruled by yesterday's pain.

Think about the daily load you carry in your mind and body. Sometimes, we describe it as tension in our shoulders or a pit in our stomach that forms whenever a specific name is mentioned or a particular memory resurfaces. These feelings are not random; they're the residue of unresolved hurts. Someone betrayed your trust, inflicted harm, or neglected you in a deep need. You absorbed that pain, believing that holding onto anger might keep you safe. But the truth is, holding onto that anger holds you captive.

Carrying anger or bitterness might feel justified—after all, if someone truly wronged you, it's normal to want recognition of their wrongdoing or restitution for what they took from you. Yet, the longer you hold onto that bitterness, the more it colors your perspective on the present. Instead of forging new, healthy relationships, you might keep everyone at arm's length, suspecting they'll hurt you too. Instead of trusting God's promise that you can flourish, you might cling to resentment, unconsciously telling yourself that letting go would excuse the offender's actions. But forgiveness is not excusing; it's freeing yourself from the punishment cycle that keeps replaying in your head.

One common misconception is that forgiveness means saying, "It's okay that you hurt me." But that's not the case at all. Forgiveness does not mean you minimize or negate the seriousness of the hurt inflicted upon you. It doesn't mean the other person escapes the consequence, or you must immediately reconcile. Some relationships can be restored after forgiveness; others cannot or should not be, depending on ongoing harm or refusal to change. At its core, forgiveness is about releasing yourself from the emotional stranglehold that bitterness maintains. Letting go of the past means refusing to allow it to dictate your present peace.

Picture bitterness as a toxin in your water supply. You keep drinking from it, day after day, convinced that you're punishing your offender by staying angry. In reality, you're poisoning your own heart. Forgiveness is filtering that toxin out—allowing the living water of healing to fill you instead. The one who hurt you might never repent, apologize, or even acknowledge what they did. Your ability to release resentment does not hinge on their actions but on your choice to reclaim your personal freedom.

For those of us rooted in faith, forgiveness finds deeper grounding in Christ's example and teachings. Throughout Scripture, we see calls to forgive "as the Lord forgave you," which can feel daunting if traumatic experiences weigh you down. After all, how can we muster that level of mercy when our spirit still stings from betrayal or violation?

Yet, God's call to forgive isn't about denying your pain; it's about trusting that divine grace can empower you to do what feels impossible. Forgiveness is, in many ways, an act of faith. You step out, whispering to your wounded soul, *"Lord, I'm still angry, but I release this hurt to You. I refuse to let it be my master any longer."* This doesn't happen in one grand moment for everyone. It can be a repeated prayer, day by day, minute by minute, especially when old memories resurface. But each time you align yourself with forgiveness, you loosen the shackles around your heart.

Before genuine forgiveness takes root, you often need to acknowledge the full extent of the hurt. Some people try to skip this step—slapping on a quick "I forgive you" without ever processing the actual damage. This can lead to suppressed emotions that eventually resurface in unhealthy ways. So, if you're still struggling to let go, pause and allow yourself to name what was taken from you: your trust, your innocence, or maybe your sense of security. Grieve those losses. Speak them aloud in prayer or write them in a journal. Let your tears flow if they need to. Mourning what was lost is part of cleansing the wound.

In these honest moments, invite God's presence. *"Lord, You see how deeply I've been hurt. Help me face this truth without being consumed by it."* The comfort of the Holy Spirit often carries you through this raw confrontation with the pain. Rather than burying or numbing it, you hold it up to the One who heals, setting the stage for a genuine release.

When you decide to forgive, you might imagine yourself carrying a heavy box labeled "Grudges" or "Anger," then setting it down on an altar, stepping back, and saying, *"I won't pick this up again."* Of course, life isn't so neat that you'll never be tempted to revisit that anger. But the act of naming that you're releasing it is powerful. Each time the temptation to stew on the hurt arises, remind yourself of that mental (or even physical) gesture: *"I already laid that down. I refuse to carry it again."*

Some people find routines helpful. You might write the offender's name or the incident on a slip of paper, pray over it, and then burn or shred it, symbolizing the choice to release. Others prefer more private expressions—like journaling a letter to the person you're forgiving, then never sending it but letting the words serve as evidence of your decision. Do what resonates with your soul; forgiveness is deeply personal. The key is to walk away from the symbolic act with a sincere intention to let go of the bitterness you once held so tightly.

After you take the step of forgiving, don't be surprised if old feelings pop up again. You might see a social media post of the person who hurt you or passes by a location that reminds you of the pain, and anger flares momentarily. This doesn't mean your forgiveness failed. It means your emotional memory still catches up to your spiritual and mental decisions. Calmly remind yourself, *"I've chosen to let this go. I refuse to dwell in resentment."* Over time, you'll find those flare-ups lose their intensity, like a wound that gradually stops throbbing once appropriately dressed.

Also, if you're dealing with an ongoing relationship—perhaps a family member or spouse still in your life—boundaries might be needed. Forgiving someone who repeatedly acts harmfully does not mean giving them unlimited access to hurt you again. You can forgive the past while still drawing lines that protect your well-being. This can include limiting contact or insisting on professional help if they're unwilling to change destructive behaviors. Far from contradicting forgiveness, boundaries uphold the truth that your dignity and safety matter and that forgiveness is not a license for abuse to continue.

When genuine forgiveness takes root in your heart, you often experience an internal unburdening. It's as though you walk a little lighter and breathe a little deeper. That heaviness of resentment that once colored every thought recedes into the background. You may still remember what happened—it's not about erasing memory—but the sting lessens, replaced by a calm acceptance. This newfound spaciousness in your soul can make room for gratitude, creativity, and even laughter you hadn't felt in years.

In a spiritual sense, forgiveness often draws you closer to God's heart. You begin to understand how His mercy operates at a deeper level. You see that just as you longed for release from bitterness; God also longs for humanity to release the shackles of vengeance and shame. Forgiveness can deepen your prayer life when you realize that the same grace that enables you to forgive also helps you navigate the complexities of any lingering pain.

Just as you have daily or weekly routines for physical or emotional health, consider forgiving and letting go an ongoing practice. Reflect on your heart periodically. Is there someone new who's offended you? A small comment that rubbed you wrong? Instead of letting bitterness fester, address it early. Pray, *"Lord, I choose to let this go. Help me respond with wisdom, not spite."* Release small hurts while they're manageable, preventing them from calcifying into deep resentments.

In turn, watch how this habit transforms your overall perspective. You become someone who proactively seeks peace. You might speak your boundaries more swiftly, resolve conflicts rather than stew on them, and maintain a spirit of grace even when people disappoint you. This doesn't mean you'll never be hurt again, but it does mean you won't carry fresh wounds for longer than necessary.

Embracing forgiveness and letting go enriches the soil of your blooming life. Imagine a plant that's been strangled by weeds of anger and grudges. The roots can stretch once you pull those weeds, and the plant can flourish in all directions. Similarly, when bitterness no longer crowds your thoughts, you have more emotional and mental bandwidth to focus on your passions, relationships, and forward momentum. You see open doors, whereas before, you only saw closed windows. You cultivate compassion for others and yourself, trusting that everyone carries hidden hurts, even as you stand firm in your dignity.

Forgiveness can spark deeper empathy. Since you know what it's like to wrestle with heartbreak, you can respond more gently to people who lash out from their woundedness. You become a vessel of healing for them, showing that while the pain is valid, it doesn't have to be a life sentence. That's how forgiveness breaks cycles of hurt, ushering in cycles of grace that spread beyond your personal story.

As you continue this blooming process, let forgiveness be your companion, not just a one-time event. Keep leaning on God's strength; let Him remind you that no matter how deep the wound, His mercies can reshape you from the inside out. Let your soul rest, knowing that you are free from the prison of unspoken grudges and that the bitterness of the past does not shape your future.

Take hold of the truth: you can move on, dream bigger, and love again. Even if the person who hurt you never acknowledges your grace, your heart's release stands valid. You've chosen to unburden yourself from a weight that was never yours to carry forever. You reclaim your present and future, stepping fully into the identity of someone who thrives, not someone forever fastened to old offenses.

Ultimately, forgiveness isn't about who was right or wrong; it's about walking the path of wholeness that God has laid out. Each time you forgive, you mirror divine compassion tangibly, reminding the world—and yourself—that redemption can blossom in places once scorched by betrayal. And as you embrace letting go, you discover a deeper well of peace, an openness to love and be loved, and a confidence that says, *"My past does not own me. I am free to bloom."* That, dear friend, is the heart of forgiveness in a life determined to flourish.

Reflection Questions

1. Who or what do you still struggle to forgive, and how is that affecting your ability to bloom?

2. How has holding onto past hurt impacted your emotional and spiritual health?

3. What misconceptions about forgiveness have kept you from fully releasing your pain?

4. What would true emotional and spiritual freedom look like for you?

5. What steps can you take today to move toward full forgiveness?

CHAPTER 6

CULTIVATING DAILY JOY

When was the last time you felt delight bubbling up inside you, unforced and free—like a gentle breeze cutting through the heat of an afternoon sun? For many who've traveled through deep trauma and emerged on the other side, joy can feel like an unexpected stranger. You might catch glimmers of it occasionally, maybe in a friendly conversation or a stunning sunset, but sustaining that sense of everyday lightness can remain elusive. You must go past those fleeting glimpses and into a life where a steady undercurrent of joy nourishes your spirit daily.

Some people wonder if joy can ever follow a history of sorrow. They recall the nightmarish chapters they've endured and question whether the shadow cast by old wounds can be fully lifted. The answer is complex and has many layers. Those scars are indeed part of your story—reminders of battles fought. But these scars do not prevent you from encountering genuine, soul-level happiness in the present. Many who have walked the darkest valleys testify that their capacity for joy has deepened because they intimately know the alternative: emptiness, fear, or despair. Embracing daily joy isn't about denying your past but deciding that your present deserves more than permanent mourning.

The Scripture tells us that "weeping may endure for a night, but joy comes in the morning." Night seasons can feel long. Some nights might stretch over months or years of your life. But dawn eventually arrives, not necessarily erasing every sorrow but warming your horizon with fresh potential. The question becomes: Will you open your heart to that warmth, allowing it to color your days, or will you remain huddled in the shadows, uncertain that you deserve the morning light?

It's vital to distinguish between joy and mere happiness. Happiness often arises from favorable external conditions, like a good meal, a pay raise, or a pleasant compliment. It tends to evaporate when circumstances change. Joy, however, has a more enduring quality rooted in a deeper wellspring. You might be in the middle of a stressful day, yet still, smile inwardly as if a gentle current of well-being flows beneath your busyness. That's joy. It's not an evasive emotion that flees the first sign of trouble; it's a steadiness that declares, "Even though I face struggles, I remain anchored in hope."

After trauma, it's easy to adopt a vigilant stance, constantly scanning the horizon for fresh threats. While that wariness once served to protect you, it can now prevent you from soaking in life's joyous moments.

Cultivating daily joy means loosening that hypervigilance, trusting that you're safe enough to delight in little blessings—a sunbeam across the floor, a friend's laughter, the satisfaction of completing a small task well. In short, you permit yourself to let good things in.

One practical way to cultivate joy is to slow down and notice the small pleasures that dot your day like seeds of color in a gray landscape. Trauma can train your mind to latch onto potential dangers, but this mindful practice trains your mind to locate the blessings. Maybe you wake up and notice the birds chirping outside your window—pause to listen. Let the melody sink in. Or when you take your first sip of coffee or tea, relish the warmth, the flavor, the comfort it brings. These micro-moments of appreciation may seem trivial, yet they accumulate into a reservoir of gratitude that counters the pull of negativity.

You can track these small joys in a simple daily journal. Jot down three things that brought delight or peaceful contentment that day. Maybe it's a friendly text message from a sibling, the satisfaction of finishing a challenging puzzle, or a verse of Scripture that resonated with your heart. By writing them down, you shift your focus from what went wrong to what went right. Over time, this process reshapes your mental landscape, fostering an outlook where joy can flourish more freely.

Trauma can weigh your soul so heavily that laughter feels frivolous or even disrespectful to the gravity of your experiences. Yet humor, in appropriate measure, can be a healing balm. It doesn't trivialize your pain; instead, it offers a counterbalance to it. Even Scripture acknowledges that "a merry heart does good like medicine." Laughter can release tension, oxygenate your body, and remind you that not every moment must be solemn.

Reintroducing humor might start with small things: watching a lighthearted show, reading a funny anecdote, or recalling a comedic memory with a friend who understands your journey. You may initially feel odd as if you're betraying the seriousness of what you endured. But allowing yourself to find amusement in everyday life is part of reclaiming your emotional spectrum—allowing brightness to exist alongside the darker hues. If you sense guilt about laughing, gently tell yourself that joy does not diminish your past struggles; it signifies that, by grace, you are expanding beyond them.

Relationships can be a rich soil for planting seeds of daily joy. You might schedule a weekly phone call with a close friend to talk about uplifting moments in your lives or practice texting each other about one positive thing that happened each day. If you're part of a faith community, maybe you join a small group to study God's Word and share personal joys and testimonies. Sometimes, hearing another person's highlight can spark a reciprocal sense of gratitude in you.

If you have a partner or live with family, consider setting aside "joy time"—perhaps after dinner, where each person quickly mentions something that made them smile. This communal habit gently reshapes the household atmosphere, reminding everyone that no matter how demanding the day is, there's still a note of goodness to be found. Over time, these small acts can shift a home's dynamic from tension or routine to an environment that breathes encouragement.

Faith can enhance joy by linking your positive moments to a loving Creator. Instead of just thinking, *"That was a lucky break,"* or *"What a pretty flower I saw in the park,"* you can pray, *"Thank You, Lord, for this blessing. Thank You for showing me beauty in ordinary life."* This practice transforms fleeting niceties into sacred reminders that God remains intimately involved in your healing and happiness.

Consider ending each day with a brief prayer of thanks—mentioning specifics like the comforting hug from a friend, the peaceful walk you took, or the sense of achievement at work. This daily spiritual discipline roots your joy in something larger than yourself, allowing it to flourish even when life's storms reemerge. You're not just noticing good things; you're attributing them to divine kindness, reinforcing a cycle of faith and gratitude.

One might worry that seeking daily joy means ignoring lingering pains or unresolved aspects of trauma. But cultivating joy doesn't call for forced positivity or denial. You can hold sorrow in one hand and joy in the other. Life's complexity includes threads of grief and gladness; wisdom lies in honoring all threads without letting sorrow overshadow the possibility of delight. This balanced view acknowledges that you may still have triggers and nights of uneasy sleep, but in tandem, you have mornings where you can intentionally choose a moment of joy to offset the gloom.

If you find yourself sliding toward an "all or nothing" mindset—thinking, *"If I'm not 100% healed, I can't be truly joyful"*—challenge that assumption. Few people reach a place of perfect wholeness. Instead, many learn to cultivate joy in the cracks of imperfection, discovering that the glow of hope can shine even through broken places. This is reminiscent of the Japanese art of kintsugi, where broken pottery is repaired with gold, making the piece more stunning because of its flaws. Let your daily joys become that gold, highlighting the beauty emerging from your scars.

Certain internal barriers might stop you from fully embracing daily joy. Guilt is a common one. You might think, *"After all I've been through, do I even have the right to be happy?"* Or, *"What about others who suffer? Isn't my joy selfish?"* Yet your joy doesn't rob empathy from those still in pain. You can remain empathetic and still let yourself breathe in life's sweetness. Experiencing daily joy can make you more compassionate because your heart brims with an overflow that can reach others.

Another barrier is the fear that joy might lead to vulnerability. *"If I let my guard down, I might be blindsided again."* Indeed, trauma taught you to keep watch for danger. But daily joy doesn't equate to being blind to risk. It's simply acknowledging that not every moment must be overshadowed by vigilance. You can keep healthy boundaries, maintain awareness, and enjoy each day's grace. This mindset shows you have evolved beyond trauma's dictates, allowing your soul a measure of release.

One practical strategy to introduce joy into your life is forming "joy routines." A routine is intentional and repeated, giving structure to your desire for daily delight. For instance, you might begin every morning by reading one uplifting quote or Scripture verse and reflecting on it for a few minutes, letting it positively frame your day. Or you might end every evening by playing a favorite soothing song and mentally recapping moments of gratitude. These routines become anchors, reminding you that joy doesn't just happen spontaneously—it can be invited, fostered, and nurtured.

Another idea is to create a "joy corner" in your home, a small space or shelf where you place items that spark delight—maybe photos of loved ones, mementos from significant breakthroughs, or a candle whose scent soothes you. When you feel drained or tense, you can step over to that spot, pause, and remind yourself of life's gentle mercies. Let it be a sanctuary of encouragement amid the day's hustle.

Interestingly, one of the richest sources of joy can be found in lifting someone else's burden. When you minister to others out of your well of compassion—be it volunteering at a local shelter, helping a neighbor with errands, or comforting a friend going through a storm—you often discover a profound sense of fulfillment. Your trauma once threatened to isolate you, but acts of service break that isolation, connecting your heart with others, and in so doing, we become part of a universal family that is sincerely empathetic.

It's not about ignoring your healing needs but recognizing that healing becomes even more vibrant when shared. You might choose a service activity that resonates with your story—like mentoring young adults who face challenges similar to what you once overcame or writing letters to survivors in crisis centers. Each small contribution helps them and deepens your sense of purpose, fueling a steady stream of joy that surpasses fleeting satisfaction.

Even with an intentional focus on cultivating joy, hard days will still appear. You might wake up agitated, haunted by dreams that dredge up old wounds, or you might face fresh stress from work or relationships. On those mornings, joy can feel like an unwelcomed guest you're too grumpy to greet. Accept that it's normal to have emotional ebbs and flows. The key is not to demand perpetual sunshine but to ensure you don't stay trapped in grayness indefinitely.

On such days, turn to the daily joys you've practiced—maybe a slow morning walk, a gratitude list, or a quick encouraging chat with a friend who knows your journey. If you still struggle, give yourself compassion: *"I'm allowed an off day, but I know tomorrow can be different. Joy isn't gone forever; it's just a bit clouded today."* That gentle self-talk prevents a temporary dip from spiraling into a crisis of faith or hope.

Joy can also be deliberately cultivated in your spiritual life. Whether through worship music, singing your heart out alone or with others, or dancing quietly in your living room as a form of praise, you invite bodily expression of the joy inside you. For some, it might be a silent reflection on God's goodness, breathing in the reality that He sees you fully, scars and all, and calls you beloved.

Scripture often portrays joy as a command: "Rejoice in the Lord always." To a trauma survivor, that might sound impossible, but when read through the lens of grace, it's more an invitation than a demand. It says, *"Step into the joy already paved for you. Even in hardship, let your heart find something worth celebrating in the presence of the One who redeems."* The difference between forcing positivity and practicing biblical joy is that the latter springs from a well of divine love, not from your attempts to deny pain.

As you continue blooming, let daily joy become your anchor and compass. On days when you feel uncertain, let joy ground you in the trust that no matter what your trauma whispered, you are indeed capable of experiencing genuine delight. Let it guide you toward choices that foster life rather than drain it—relationships that nurture your best self, activities that awaken your creativity, and faith practices that infuse every breath with hope.

Imagine a garden that's been carefully tended over time: once barren soil, now teeming with vibrant flowers. That's the metaphor for your heart, once overshadowed by sorrow, now increasingly radiant. You might still have pockets of weeds or occasional pests—remnants of old triggers or doubts—but the landscape is changing. Joy helps keep those unwanted elements in check, ensuring they don't regain dominion.

Don't keep your joy to yourself. When you find it, please share it with those around you who might still be stuck in the desert of despair. Your laugh, genuine smile, and encouraging words can ignite hope in hearts that barely remember what hope feels like. Joy is contagious in the best sense: others see the light in your eyes and wonder, *"If they, with all they've faced, can still embrace daily joy, maybe I can too."* In that sense, your daily delight becomes a testimony of your resilience and God's redemptive hand in your life.

Some folks may question your new buoyancy—*"Don't you remember what happened?"* They might think you're in denial. But you'll know the truth: joy coexists with the memory of pain, shining because you refused to let pain be the final chapter. Let your joy stand as a beacon, a statement that life after trauma isn't just survival but can unfold into abundant living.

As you near the end of this chapter, reflect on how daily joy can shape your next steps. Perhaps you'll refine your daily routine, ensuring there's room every morning to savor a personal delight, be it a Scripture reading or a few stolen minutes of quiet reflection. Maybe you'll commit to writing a "joy note" once a week to a friend, celebrating something positive they bring to your life. Even incorporating playful breaks—like taking a walk for no reason other than watching clouds—can be transformative.

Over time, these practices weave joy into the fabric of your everyday experiences. Trauma once forced you to keep your guard up. Now, you lower that guard a bit, letting the sunshine in. Yes, you remain wise—trauma teaches you not to be naïve—but you no longer let caution eclipse your chance to experience delight. That balanced perspective—guarded but open, wise but still trusting—is part of what it means to bloom after pain.

Cultivating daily joy is about turning small moments into seeds of grace that grow within you, no matter what else you face. Seeing life through a lens of possibility rather than resignation is an ongoing decision. You nurture a soul that radiates warmth despite scars by consistently anchoring in gratitude, humor, kindness to others, and faith's unwavering promise.

So go ahead: wake up tomorrow and look for something that makes you smile—a bird perched on a windowsill, a verse that speaks hope, or the face of someone who cares. Let that smile take root in your heart, letting you breathe lighter throughout the day. Then, please do it again the next day and the day after. Before long, you'll discover that joy is no stranger—it's become your morning companion, midday friend, and solace at night. And in that sweet abiding, you truly bloom, shining from the inside out with a joy proclaiming, *"I have survived, and I am living again in full color."*

Reflection Questions

1. What small joys have you overlooked in your daily life?

2. How does fear of disappointment keep you from fully embracing joy?

3. What practices can you incorporate to make joy a part of your daily routine?

4. How does gratitude shift your perspective, even in difficult times?

5. How can you intentionally choose joy, even when circumstances don't change?

Chapter 7
Stepping Into New Opportunities

When a flower finally opens its petals to the morning sun, it isn't just displaying its vibrant colors. It's also making a silent declaration: I have survived the storms, the night, the darkness, and the isolation. I have pushed through the soil and am ready to greet the day. In the same way, stepping into new opportunities after seasons of trauma and healing represents an inner unveiling of who you have become. No longer shackled by the same fears that once paralyzed you, you're now poised at the threshold of possibility. I encourage you to embrace that threshold, to say yes when life extends fresh invitations, and to trust that you can thrive in uncharted territory.

Perhaps you've noticed a stirring within you—a sense that while your healing journey has been substantial, you're eager for something beyond just being "okay." Maybe you sense a calling to a new career path, a desire to deepen your involvement in ministry, or a longing to finally chase a dream once shelved due to trauma's heavy hand. That longing is often the Spirit's nudge, whispering that there is more to you than simply managing your wounds day by day. There comes a time in the healing process when survival mode no longer fits, and your soul aches for new frontiers.

Yet wanting more can feel unsettling if you've grown used to the safety net of predictability. Trauma can teach us to keep our world small to avoid further pain. But keeping life small also shrinks your capacity for joy, growth, and impact. Stepping into new opportunities means accepting a certain level of risk: *What if I fail? What if people reject me again? What if this new venture reopens old wounds?* These questions can swirl like a whirlwind in your mind, but there's risk in every bold move of faith. And it's that risk that often births fresh purpose.

Look for signs of divine orchestration when you stand on the verge of something new. Maybe you start noticing a recurring theme in sermons or conversations that point you toward a specific direction—like volunteering, a new creative project, or leadership in your community. Or a door suddenly opens to enroll in a class that's always intrigued you. These so-called coincidences may be gentle God-incidences, inviting you to step beyond your comfort zone.

Discernment matters here. You don't want to chase every glittering possibility without prayerful reflection. Sometimes, the enemy of our souls tries to lure us into distractions that keep us busy but not necessarily fruitful. So, weigh opportunities: Does this new path align with your values, healing progress, and the unique gifts God has placed in you? Does it excite your spirit, even if it scares you a bit? Faith thrives in the interplay between excitement and reverent caution. That tension often indicates you're standing in front of a door that could expand your horizons.

Just because you're healing doesn't mean doubt won't try to sabotage your new beginnings. Old tapes may play, whispering, *"You're not qualified enough," "You'll only get hurt again,"* or *"Who are you to try something big?"* These echoes of past trauma can threaten to hold you back from stepping into the abundant life God envisions for you. Recognizing this inner critic is half the battle. The other half is responding to it with truth.

Remind yourself of how far you've come. You've built resilience, practiced new coping mechanisms, and encountered the sustaining presence of God along the way. If you've grown this much since your days of deepest wounding, imagine the fruit that might grow if you plant yourself in new territory now. Doubt may not vanish overnight, but each time it rears its head, anchor your mind in Scripture: "God has not given us a spirit of fear but of power, love, and a sound mind." Rest in that power, that love, and that clarity as you contemplate fresh avenues.

Sometimes, a new opportunity appears intimidating—a significant career shift or a big leap in personal ministry. Instead of plunging in all at once, break it down. If you want to start a nonprofit organization to support trauma survivors, you don't have to file the paperwork tomorrow. Begin by researching existing charities, volunteering in a related sphere, or chatting with people who've done similar work. If you want to write a book about your healing journey, start with shorter reflective pieces or devotions for a small audience. These small steps build your confidence and hone your skills, ensuring that when you make a bigger move, you're fortified by tangible experience.

This gradual approach also helps you gauge your emotional readiness. If you are overwhelmed, you should revisit specific healing tools or seek additional support. On the other hand, if each small step invigorates you, that's a sign you're moving in sync with your divine calling. The key is forward motion—even if it's slow. The inertia of a single action often opens the door to the next, building momentum that transforms apprehension into excitement.

No new venture is immune to setbacks. You might apply for a dream job, face rejection, or attempt a new hobby, only to stumble initially. Trauma survivors can be susceptible to perceived failures, seeing them as confirmation of deep-seated fears. But remember, resilience is part of your new identity. A setback doesn't negate your progress; it's an invitation to learn, adapt, and try again.

When you run into a snag, bring your disappointment before God. Pray something like, *"Lord, I feel discouraged right now, but I'm surrendering this outcome to You. Show me how to recalibrate and strengthen my resolve."* Then consult mentors or trusted friends who can speak wisdom into your situation. Let them remind you that one closed door might steer you toward a better opportunity or that your calling remains valid even if you need to refine your approach.

As you say yes to new opportunities, remember that healing from trauma has taught you the importance of boundaries and pacing. In your eagerness to bloom, you could overcommit or become so focused on your fresh pursuits that you neglect self-care. True flourishing involves balance: investing in new ventures while maintaining the rest, relationships, and spiritual disciplines that keep you stable.

Before accepting a big project or role, ask yourself: *Do I have the emotional bandwidth right now? Will this commitment undermine my daily routines of calm and reflection?* Sometimes, a delay or a scaled-back version of your dream might be the wiser path if it respects your healing. Blooming doesn't mean sprinting in all directions at once. It means unfolding gracefully, letting each petal open in its proper time. God's plan for you isn't a frantic race; it's a journey of intentional steps.

Faith becomes both a compass and an engine as you navigate new opportunities. A compass because it orients you toward God's voice over the noise of random ideas. An engine because it propels you forward, fueling you with confidence that the One who led you out of trauma continues to guide your future. Without faith, you might falter at the first sign of resistance or confusion. With faith, you press on, assured that if you remain pliable in God's hands, He'll lead you into the open fields where your gifts can flourish.

Cultivating this faith might involve a morning prayer: *"Lord, open my eyes to the doors You want me to walk through and close those that would hinder my growth."* It might also involve an evening journaling session, reflecting on how the day's events resonate with your sense of calling.

Over time, these practices deepen your sensitivity to divine direction, helping you sift through opportunities that sparkle but might not be aligned with your long-term well-being.

In stepping into new opportunities, it helps to learn from those who've tread a similar path. Maybe you can talk to a friend who shifted careers midlife, a church leader who expanded a ministry, or a mentor who turned personal adversity into a platform of service.

Listening to their stories also provides practical insights. They might share cautionary tales about pitfalls to avoid or tips for managing time, relationships, and resources as you pursue your calling. In your healing journey, you likely experienced the power of community; the same principle applies here. You don't have to navigate brand-new territory alone. Surround yourself with wise counsel, allowing the experiences of others to shape your approach so you can advance with humility and boldness.

Trauma can create regrets—like lost opportunities, derailed plans, or crumbled relationships. Moving into new opportunities sometimes stirs old sadness about what you previously missed. But remember, God is a God of second chances (and third, fourth, etc.). This fresh opportunity might be a divine do-over, a chance to reclaim aspects of your life that felt stolen. Even if it looks different now—maybe you're older, your environment has changed, or your perspective is more nuanced—it can still represent a form of redemption.

Embracing second chances calls for grace. You aren't the same person who once made fearful decisions or let an opportunity slip by. Maybe you're seasoned by your healing. Approach these do-overs with the tenderness that says, "I'm grateful for another shot. I'm committed to approaching this with wisdom, remembering the lessons of my past." This gentle acceptance of second chances transforms lingering shame into gratitude, fueling your momentum toward the new horizon.

Consider how your story might influence others as you step into new opportunities. Survival mode is inherently self-focused—you do what you must to keep afloat. But once you move into bloom, you often discover a latent desire to help others grow. Perhaps you sense a calling to mentor younger folks, share your faith journey on a podcast or blog, or volunteer in a community project that addresses an issue close to your heart. These aren't just random ideas; they reflect the outpouring of what you've cultivated within.

Stepping into new opportunities can shift from personal ambition to a communal blessing. As you fulfill your potential, your life becomes a testimony, a living parable of how darkness can yield to light and how sorrow can evolve into steadfast joy. You might never see the full ripple effect of your influence, but rest assured it's there—every open door you walk through can open another door for someone looking at you, seeing hope in your footsteps.

Not every day on this new path will glow with excitement. Some days will feel mundane or confusing, making you question whether you heard God's call or your aspirations were misplaced. In those moments, resilience and faith come into play yet again. Reflect on how, even during your healing, you faced setbacks but learned to pivot, adapt, and keep going. The same principle applies when forging into new territory. A project might stall, a relationship might not yield the collaboration you expected, or an opportunity might dissolve unexpectedly.

Every drawback eventually makes room for a new flow. The key is to remain teachable, letting each disappointment refine your perspective rather than derail your vision. If a door slams, ask God to reveal another opening or redirect your talents where they can truly flourish. This fluid posture—holding your dreams but not clutching them so tightly that you can't adjust—ensures you grow in flexibility and faithfulness.

As you once learned to celebrate small victories in your healing, apply that principle to your new ventures. Volunteering for a charity and helping one person see a glimpse of hope is a breakthrough worth acknowledging. If you pitch a creative idea at work and your boss nods and says, "Let's explore that," it's a seed planted in fresh soil. Overlooking these mini-breakthroughs can rob you of the joy and motivation needed to sustain your forward motion.

So, take time to mark these moments. You might journal about them, share them with a supportive friend, or whisper a prayer of thanks: *"Lord, I see the small fruit you're allowing me to bear. I'm grateful for the chance to serve or create."* By celebrating each milestone—no matter how modest—you keep your heart engaged, your mind inspired, and your faith thriving in the face of the unknown.

A crucial aspect of stepping into new opportunities is avoiding the trap of living perpetually in the future—always looking for that next big break. Your healing taught you the value of being present, noticing your feelings, and acknowledging each day's mercies. Carry that lesson with you as you venture out. Ambition can be healthy, but not if it consumes your capacity to appreciate the here and now. Sometimes, you'll need to pause your hustle, take a breath, and remember how good it is to be alive, how remarkable it is that you're even in a position to seek fresh horizons after all you've endured.

You can sense God's delight in your progress in these quiet pauses. You realize that beyond chasing achievements, the real treasure is found in the process—how your character is shaped, your reliance on grace deepens, and your soul remains anchored in sincerity and love. New opportunities, then, become not merely ends in themselves but avenues through which your healed heart can express its wholeness.

As you stand on this threshold, poised to say yes to what life (and God) might be opening before you, take a moment to remember the journey from scarred to mended and now to blooming. That arc of transformation is your backdrop, evidence that you can do hard things, adapt, survive, and then flourish. If the new opportunity feels daunting, recall the nights you thought you'd never see another sunrise of hope—and you did. Recall the triggers you once couldn't bear but now only faintly rattle you. *This* is evidence that stepping into unfamiliar territory, while scary, can also be profoundly rewarding.

You might slip at times or question your readiness. That's normal. But hold onto the truth: your life story did not culminate in trauma, nor did it end at mere functional healing. It's now expanding into purpose, service, creativity, or leadership—whatever form your next opportunity takes. Faith remains your bedrock, reminding you that even if you fall, the God who carried you this far won't abandon you. As you sow your gifts and time into new fields, trust that the seeds will produce a harvest in season—maybe in ways you can't even foresee.

Stepping into new opportunities encapsulates the spirit of *Bloom*. It says, "I've tended my wounds, I've grown my roots of faith, and now I'm ready to extend my branches beyond the edge of what I once believed possible." This chapter of your life is a gateway, not just a final step. You'll encounter fresh lessons, challenges, and joys through each door you walk. You'll extend your capacity to love, influence, and be shaped by God's grace.

Embrace each invitation with humble confidence, acknowledging that you don't have to be perfect to enter new spaces. You only need to be willing to try, learn, lean on faith, and see how your evolving heart can impact the world around you. You no longer stand as the wounded soul who couldn't imagine a future. You stand as a beloved child of God, marked by resilience, fueled by hope, and ready for the sunshine of tomorrow.

So let your roots hold fast, nourished by all you've discovered in your healing. Let your leaves reach out, soaking in the inspiration and opportunities God places along your path. And let your blossoms unfold in vibrant testimony that a life once cast in darkness can bloom in radiant color, stepping boldly into all that awaits.

Reflection Questions

1. What opportunities have you avoided out of fear or self-doubt?

2. How does stepping out in faith challenge your comfort zone?

3. What gifts or talents have you been hesitant to use?

4. How do you see God preparing you for something greater than what you imagined?

5. What is one opportunity you need to say "yes" to today?

Chapter 8

Becoming a Source of Encouragement

Maria hadn't stepped foot in her backyard in over a year. The garden her grandmother had once tended with love had turned into a graveyard of brittle stems and lifeless soil. Weeds choked the empty spaces where roses used to bloom, a mirror of how Maria felt inside—withered, abandoned, forgotten. But one morning, after months of numbing silence, she picked up a watering can. At first, it felt pointless. What good could a few drops do in the face of so much ruin? But she poured anyway—day after day. Little by little, the soil softened, and fragile green shoots began to push through the dirt. She hadn't realized it, but as she revived the garden, something inside her was coming back to life, too. Healing wasn't instant. It wasn't effortless. But it was real. And as those first blossoms opened, Maria understood—her journey wasn't just about survival. It was about showing others that even the most barren places could bloom again.

So many souls wander in valleys of despair, battered by experiences they barely speak of. They look around, unsure if anyone can fathom their weight or point them to a path of renewal. Yet here you stand, a testament that it is possible to rise from the darkest nights. Being a source of encouragement involves sharing that glimmer of hope. It doesn't demand perfection or a loud platform; it only requires a compassionate willingness to say, "I've been there, and there is a way forward."

Trauma often isolates people, convincing them that their pain is singular and their burdens incommunicable. In this state of isolation, even small acts of kindness or empathy can shift the trajectory of someone's recovery. Encouragement is more than telling someone to "hang in there" or spouting optimistic phrases. It's about witnessing someone else's struggle, looking them in the eye, and validating their feelings. It's also about offering the perspective that brokenness does not have to be the final chapter.

When you step in as an encourager, you're helping to rewrite the narrative they've come to believe about themselves. Maybe they've concluded they're unlovable, or that hope is an illusion. A few heartfelt words from you—rooted in your own story of rising above deep wounds—can plant seeds of possibility in their heart's barren soil. Encouragement invites them to consider that if transformation was possible for you, it might be possible for them.

Before you can effectively encourage others, it's important to acknowledge your scars and the healing process that brought you here. Your scars are not a liability; they are evidence that you've walked through the valley and come out carrying valuable knowledge. Think of them as credentials: not the sort you boast about, but the kind that say, "I understand because I've felt this. Let's find a way forward."

This doesn't mean you have to have all your issues solved. Encouragement does not require that you be fully healed. You only need to be on the road, gleaning enough hope and lessons to share with those a few steps behind. The humility of admitting, "I'm still in the process myself, yet I've discovered certain truths that can help," often makes your encouragement more believable. People sense authenticity in humility; they resonate with someone who gets the messiness of healing rather than presenting a glossy facade of perfection.

Sometimes, the most tremendous encouragement you can offer isn't a stirring pep talk but a quiet, attentive ear. Many who suffer in silence need someone to validate their story—someone who won't flinch or change the subject when they mention their nightmares or bursts of anxiety. By patiently hearing them, you communicate, *"Your experiences matter, and you're not alone in them."*

You might recall desperately needing a space to speak without being judged in those listening moments. As you provide that space for someone else, you become a healing presence. It's not about having perfect advice. It's about letting them unburden themselves and trusting that the Holy Spirit can work through your compassionate silence as much as your words. After all, encouragement is often felt more intensely in witnessing than lecturing.

Sometimes, your words—specifically your story—hold transformative potential. People learn from real-life examples. They can glean hope from your journey's arc if they know you battled severe anxiety or overcame betrayal. Telling your story doesn't require fancy rhetoric; honesty is enough. Share the lows as well as the turning points. Please talk about your fear and the measures you took to unravel it. Most importantly, emphasize the redemptive threads: how you found resilience, how God's grace surprised you when you least expected it, and how each small victory led to the bigger picture of blooming.

Still, caution is essential. You don't want to overshadow someone else's story or inadvertently cause them to feel small. The spotlight should remain on God's faithfulness and the principle that healing is possible, not on your strength alone. Telling your testimony works best when it's shaped with empathy—meaning you tailor what you share to the listener's situation. If they're in deep grief, dwell on the portion of your story where you felt raw and uncertain, letting them know it's normal to feel that way. Provide glimpses of how you coped in that stage rather than skipping straight to your triumphs.

Encouragement extends beyond words. Sometimes, a simple service gesture can speak volumes to someone whose life feels battered. Maybe it's preparing a meal for a neighbor who's overwhelmed by depression or stress. Perhaps it's offering to babysit for a single parent who rarely gets a break. Or volunteering to drive a friend to counseling sessions if transportation is a barrier. These practical acts say, "I see your struggle, and I'm willing to lighten your load."

For those who have endured trauma, receiving help can feel awkward at first, as they might be used to self-reliance or isolation. Having walked a parallel journey, you can gently stand in the gap, reminding them that accepting help doesn't equate to weakness. Through these acts, you embody the compassion you once craved. Over time, consistent kindness can soften their defenses, possibly paving the way for deeper conversations or spiritual breakthroughs.

If you're part of a family or faith community, your influence can help shape an atmosphere where encouragement thrives. This might involve hosting small gatherings focusing on mutual support, where each person shares one challenge and victory, and the rest respond with empathy and prayer. Or you could suggest a "praise wall" in a communal space, where members post notes about breakthroughs or blessings they've encountered.

In your home, you could institute a "highlight of the day" routine, where each member names a positive moment from their day before bedtime. Such routines don't deny the reality of ongoing trauma or stress. They shift the cultural norm from a negative default to one that regularly spotlights hope and forward momentum. In these ways, encouragement becomes woven into the group's identity, not just an occasional nicety.

Trauma doesn't discriminate based on culture, background, or language. You might find yourself in a position to encourage someone with a very different life experience from your own. This can feel intimidating—how do you speak into a struggle you don't fully grasp? But compassion and listening transcend cultural barriers. The language of empathy resonates beyond differences in tradition or worldview.

When bridging cultural gaps, remain open and curious. Ask questions about their perspective, family dynamics, or spiritual beliefs. Show respect for what might be an unfamiliar heritage and humbly share your own story, acknowledging where your experiences diverge and where they might overlap. Avoid imposing your coping methods as a one-size-fits-all remedy; invite them to glean what resonates from your testimony, trusting that the Holy Spirit can adapt the lessons to their unique context.

While stepping into the role of encourager is powerful, it also demands self-awareness. If you plunge too deeply into someone else's pain, you risk being pulled under, reactivating your wounds, or leading to compassion fatigue. The aim is to let your empathy guide you, not consume you. Remember how vital boundaries were in your healing? They remain crucial here. You can care deeply for someone while still safeguarding your well-being.

Check in with yourself periodically. Are you feeling drained from carrying too many of others' burdens? Are you losing focus on your daily practices that keep you grounded—like prayer, quiet time, or safe peer support? If so, scale back and refresh. Encourage them to seek professional help if their needs exceed what a friend or spiritual companion can provide. Genuine encouragement doesn't mean ignoring your limits; it means partnering with them in a healthy manner that's sustainable for both of you.

Encouragement can sometimes veer into empty positivity if not balanced with honesty. The last thing a person dealing with trauma or adversity needs is a barrage of clichés that deny their pain or oversimplify their struggle. The encouragement that truly heals includes acknowledging the gravity of what they face while still shining a beacon of hope. Instead of saying, "Everything happens for a reason," which might sound dismissive, you might say, "I don't have all the answers for why this happened, but I believe your future can hold more than this pain." This approach respects their weight without letting it overshadow the possibility of transformation.

Likewise, be mindful not to place unhelpful burdens on them by implying they need to "pray harder." Yes, prayer is vital, but so is therapy, rest, supportive relationships, and the slow, patient work of processing trauma. By encouraging from a place of sincerity and integrated wisdom, you offer them a more complete picture of healing's multifaceted nature. Compassion means seeing them as a whole person—body, mind, and spirit—and guiding them to resources that can address each dimension.

Being a source of encouragement doesn't just uplift others—it enriches your ongoing blooming process. As you invest in someone's journey, you reinforce your lessons, remembering how each principle of healing played out in your story. Their struggles might remind you of where you've been, prompting gratitude for how far you've come. You may glean new perspectives or see fresh reasons to keep pressing forward. It becomes a beautiful cycle: your healing fosters empathy and encouragement, reinforcing your healing.

Scripture often speaks of comforting others with the same comfort we've received from God. That reciprocal model ensures that the gifts you've harvested from adversity do not remain idle. They're poured back into the community, forging connections of grace. You find that your bloom extends beyond self-satisfaction into a ministry of presence—where your existence testifies that redemption is authentic, accessible, and ongoing.

How do you maintain this role without burning out? First, keep feeding your soul. Return to the daily practices that stabilize your journey: prayer, reflection, grounding techniques, or spiritual fellowship. Keep your lines of communication open with mentors or trusted companions who can remind you that while it's healthy to pour out, you also need refilling. Lean on God in prayer regularly, acknowledging that you can't carry everyone's burdens indefinitely. You do your part and trust His grace to handle the rest.

Additionally, practice discernment. Not everyone will be open to the help you're eager to give, and that's okay. Some might reject your overtures or cling to a victim mindset. Offer empathy, but recognize you can't force healing upon them. Encouragement thrives on receptivity. Where receptivity is absent, you can still love them from a gentle distance, praying that one day they'll be ready to receive what you and God's Spirit might offer.

As you continue encouraging those still in the trenches, you help birth a new generation of encouragers. Think of it as passing the torch to others who can turn around and shine a light on someone else's path once they get a foothold in their healing. This ripple effect may spread beyond your immediate circle. It might reach entire families, communities, or online circles across geographical boundaries. The seeds you plant by simply affirming someone's worth can sprout into entire movements of hope.

You might never see the full impact of these seeds, but that's the nature of sowing encouragement. Some might blossom in a year, others in a decade, and may reach places you never travel. The point is you're acting out of faith, trusting the multiplier effect of grace. Your role is cultivating relationships with love, sincerity, and the wisdom gleaned from your healing story, leaving the outcome to the divine gardener.

Let's reflect on the joy of being a source of encouragement. Trauma once tried to lock you in isolation, shame, and fear. But your progress has unlocked a capacity to speak life into others. Whenever you witness a spark of hope rekindling in someone's eyes, you taste a joy that any self-centered pursuit can't manufacture. It's the joy of purposeful connection—of seeing how your scars become road signs for a fellow traveler searching for a way out of their pain.

This joy doesn't vanish the moment you stop speaking. It echoes in your prayers, the next steps that person takes, and the overall beauty of your life. You realize that healing wasn't only about you feeling better; it was also about you stepping into a realm where your experiences could serve a far greater purpose. That is the essence of living in bloom: your healing yields fruit that nourish the weary lifts the downcast and testifies to the unstoppable force of redemption.

Becoming a source of encouragement is not a separate track from your healing journey; it's a continuation of it. You can't give what you haven't internalized. The compassion, hope, and faith you share with others reflect the seeds that have taken root in your soul. And as you pour out, you find yourself increasingly open to the gentle rains of grace that sustain your bloom.

Never doubt that your words, your listening ear, your presence in someone else's crisis, can shift the trajectory of their life. You stand as living proof that darkness doesn't claim the final word. So take courage: keep your heart attuned to those who wander in shadows, speak love into their confusion, and watch how encouragement transforms both the giver and the receiver. In doing so, you fully embody this stage of your journey, showing that a life once battered can indeed blossom—and, in its blooming, scatter seeds of hope across the fields of a broken world.

Reflection Questions

1. Who in your life needs the encouragement you once needed?

2. How has your journey through pain positioned you to lift others?

3. In what ways can your testimony bring hope to someone else?

4. What fears keep you from sharing your story, and how can you overcome them?

5. How can you intentionally be a light in someone else's healing journey?

Chapter 9

Continuing to Bloom

When you first stepped into this season of blooming, you might have expected a grand finale—a day where you'd declare yourself fully healed, free from every scar's echo. But real growth rarely wraps up with a neat little bow. Instead, it reveals new buds and branches whenever you think you've reached your peak. *Continuing to Bloom* is about realizing that the transformation you began doesn't stop when you feel somewhat stable. It keeps unfolding like petals in the morning sun, inviting you into deeper levels of purpose and wholeness than you once thought possible.

Perhaps you can recall a time in your healing when you thought, *"If I can just get past these triggers, I'll be done."* Or, *"Once I trust people again, that's it—I'm fixed."* But healing seldom stands still. As you peel back layers of pain, new layers appear, each with its lessons and breakthroughs. The good news is that each stage brings unexpected joys and revelations about your strengths.

Think of a tree in different seasons: it buds in spring, blossoms in summer, and sheds leaves in autumn—but the roots keep growing year-round. Even in winter's stillness, life stirs beneath the bark. You, too, might appear stable on the outside, but inside, deeper roots are stretching into fresh soil, ensuring you remain anchored through changing times. This ongoing blooming process might feel intimidating if you crave a finish line, but it also testifies to the vast potential God placed within you.

Continuing to bloom means embracing a mindset of perpetual discovery. You won't always be locked in intense emotional labor—some phases will be gentler, letting you enjoy your progress. But you'll likely encounter periods where old pains resurface, or new challenges arise, prompting further growth. Rather than labeling it as a regression, see it as a continuing spiral upward. You've circled this terrain before, but from a higher vantage point, you respond with deeper wisdom and renewed faith.

It's easy to look at triggers or moments of discomfort and think, *"I guess I'm still broken."* But if you assess carefully, you'll realize you handle them differently now. Maybe you calm your breath instead of spiraling into a panic. Perhaps you speak your needs instead of swallowing them out of fear. Such shifts indicate that your capacity for resilience and self-love has expanded.

Allow yourself to celebrate these "micro-upgrades." Each time you choose a healthier response and reframe a negative thought, you're effectively living out a new layer of healing. Where once you dreaded the day's stress, you might tackle it with measured faith and improved coping. These small victories deserve recognition, not because you're boasting but because you are acknowledging the ongoing miracle of transformation. It's like seeing fresh petals appear on a plant you once assumed was done flowering. The more you recognize such moments, the more motivation you gain to keep pressing forward.

In the early stages of healing, faith might have been your lifeline to survive the storms—crying out to God in your darkest hours. As you move into a season of continued blooming, faith can evolve from a desperate plea into a steady relationship of communion. You might find yourself asking for comfort and listening for God's direction. Faith transitions from rescue to partnership, where you begin building a life that mirrors divine purpose.

Try integrating spiritual disciplines in new ways. Perhaps you experiment with contemplative prayer, letting your heart dwell quietly in God's presence without an agenda. Or you might dive deeper into Scripture, seeking passages that speak to healing and the fruitfulness God envisions for your life. Some find that journaling prayers or theological reflections awaken fresh insights. Whatever your approach, ensure that faith remains a conversation, not a monologue. Because as you continue blooming, the questions shift from *"Lord, will I survive?"* to *"Lord, how shall I thrive in your plan?"*

When trauma dominated your story, you may have shrunk your aspirations, convinced that specific dreams were out of reach. As you stand stronger, you might sense a push to revisit those dreams or explore entirely new ones. Start a creative venture, lead a small group, or embark on a career path that aligns with your renewed purpose.

Stepping into these dreams requires courage. Trauma might whisper, *"Who do you think you are to aim so high?"* But the journey you've walked—the resilience you've built—is your qualification. By continuing to bloom, you trust that the same grace that carried you through darkness will empower you to expand your horizons. Keep your eyes open for unexpected doors, people who affirm your gifts, and an inner conviction that you're ready for the next step. Just remember to pace yourself. Blooming doesn't mean you have to become everything overnight. Let the momentum of healing guide you at a sustainable rhythm.

Relationships play a crucial role in continual bloom. Like a plant that benefits from companion planting, your growth is nurtured by a supportive network. That includes fellow survivors, mentors, spiritual leaders, and new friends who embrace the blossoming you rather than clinging to your wounded past. Lean into these connections. Share your evolving story with them, reciprocate when they share theirs, and celebrate each other's milestones.

Yet, also remain mindful that old dynamics might attempt to stifle your new growth. Some people in your life might prefer the version of you that stayed silent or didn't dream too big. They might unintentionally sabotage your forward momentum out of their insecurities or fears. Part of continuing to bloom involves discerning which relationships foster life and which relationships hinder your flourishing. That doesn't always mean cutting people off entirely but setting boundaries that protect your newfound expansion. Sometimes, simply limiting specific conversations or refusing to revisit old conflicts can preserve your progress.

After crossing significant healing milestones, it's tempting to ease up on self-care, thinking you don't need it as intensely. But old stress patterns can sneak back if you neglect the basic practices that steadied you—like mindful breathing, journaling, or counseling check-ins. Blooming is not about discarding the scaffolding that helped you rebuild; it's about integrating those habits into a lifestyle that sustains your well-being.

Take a moment to reevaluate your self-care regimen for this new phase. Perhaps your triggers have lessened, so you don't need the same level of daily grounding. But that doesn't mean you abandon grounding altogether. Instead, you might incorporate a weekly mental health "audit," where you quickly assess how your heart feels, how your body is doing, and whether you need a short spiritual retreat or a conversation with a trusted friend. This approach ensures that your blossoming isn't cut short by avoidable pitfalls.

Additionally, consider adding a celebratory dimension to your self-care: treat yourself to an afternoon in nature, a hobby class, or a mini-vacation when feasible. You're not just surviving anymore; you're living. These small indulgences can reinforce to your spirit that life can hold joy without guilt and that investing in your happiness is a legitimate part of your journey.

Continuing to bloom doesn't immunize you from adversity. Life will still throw curveballs—financial stress, relational conflicts, health issues. The difference is that you now face them from a stronger, more rooted place. Rather than seeing each new challenge as a threat to your bloom, see it as an opportunity to deepen your roots further. This perspective shift transforms trials into stepping stones of growth instead of stumbling blocks that drag you back into the shadows of trauma.

For instance, if a conflict arises at work, recall how you once navigated mistrust triggers. Use the communication skills you honed in therapy or personal reflection. If a friend's betrayal stings you, you might find you can address it calmly or set boundaries without being consumed by old feelings of helplessness. Even if the challenge initially rattles you, the recovery time is quicker. You bounce back, reinforced by the knowledge that storms no longer define you.

As you mature in this continual bloom, be mindful of the ripple effect on those around you. Family members, coworkers, or acquaintances might observe how you handle stress or engage with life's opportunities. Your story—once steeped in trauma—can now serve as a living testament to the possibility of redemption. People might approach you, asking how you found the courage to love again or how you manage anxiety with such poise.

Sharing your testimony isn't about boasting. It's about letting hope spread. You don't have to volunteer every painful detail unless it feels appropriate. Sometimes, a simple statement, "I went through some tough times, but by God's grace and some steady work, I've discovered life can indeed move forward," speaks volumes. That short statement can plant a seed of possibility in someone else's journey, sparking them to seek similar healing. In this way, you become a beacon—not because you flaunt your healing, but because you embody hope without pretense.

There are subtle indicators that you're not merely out of survival mode but thriving in your expanded life. Maybe you find yourself naturally setting career goals, personal achievements, or ministry aims that you once dismissed as unattainable. Or you notice your attitude toward relationships shifting from defensive to open, from waiting to be hurt to looking for mutual enrichment. You might also sense a deeper attunement with your spiritual life, feeling God's prompting more clearly or stepping forward to serve others with less reservation.

In practical terms, you might feel a shift in daily rhythms: more laughter, more spontaneous acts of kindness, or a simpler time enjoying quiet joys like reading a good book or gardening. These small daily fruits attest to the harvest your continued bloom is producing. They reveal a life that's not just free from trauma's tight grip but actively radiant with a peace that surpasses understanding. They're glimpses of how your life, once weighed down by scars, is now brimming with fresh color and purpose.

You might still ask, *"When will I be done blooming?"* The honest answer is that growth—especially the kind that emerges from deep healing—doesn't have a final endpoint. There's no finish line in faith or personal development. As you explore new fields of calling or new relationships, you'll uncover deeper facets of your character and realize new ways you can refine your walk. That doesn't mean you'll be in perpetual struggle; instead, there's always more of God's grace to discover, your resilience to strengthen, and more fruit to bear.

Once you accept this perpetual growth, it can feel liberating. It frees you from striving for some elusive "perfect" state and lets you dwell in a posture of ongoing learning. You become like a tree that keeps adding rings each year, each telling a story of the seasons you weathered. Some rings might reflect harsh conditions but show survival, adaptation, and maturity.

As you continue this journey, remember that storms might revisit. Changes in life—job transitions, health crises, or new emotional complexities—can momentarily test the solidity of your bloom. But each time, you return to the foundation you've laid: the coping tools, the faith that anchored you, the community that supports you. Trust that God, who brought you through your darkest nights, will not withdraw His presence when fresh clouds appear.

Also, hold onto a sense of expectancy. The best might still be ahead. Who's to say what doors will open as you present your authentic, healing self to the world? You might stumble upon a ministry that resonates deeply or forge a friendship that transforms your life and theirs. Keeping your heart receptive lets your blossoming soul connect to opportunities that align with your renewed identity.

Continuing to bloom is an act of faith that says, *"I will not settle for partial recovery or half-hearted living. I will keep expanding, trusting, and showing up in a world that needs real testimonies of hope."* Once you gripped the edges of your survival, you can now navigate life's complexities with an openness that fosters more profound relationships and purposeful endeavors.

Let your life preach the message that trauma may mar a season, but it cannot define an entire existence. Through your daily decisions to remain open to growth, you exemplify how life, once battered, can radiate genuine beauty. This posture of ongoing transformation also serves as a constant invitation for others to step onto their path of blossoming. By merely living out your continued bloom with courage and humility, you model a possibility for those still wrestling in the dark: that they, too, can sprout leaves of faith and blossoms of joy, no matter how bleak their past.

Finally, celebrate the chapters you've already conquered. Give thanks for the seeds that have sprouted into well-rooted plants. I look forward to the new buds that will open in the seasons still ahead. In life's grand design, a soul that continues to bloom never ceases to reveal more beauty, fruit, and evidence that broken ground can yield the most stunning gardens—when nurtured by faith, perseverance, and unending grace.

Reflection Questions

1. What does "blooming" mean to you at this stage of your life?

2. How can you maintain the progress you've made without slipping back into old patterns?

3. What habits or mindsets do you need to continue nurturing to thrive long-term?

4. How will you remind yourself that healing is an ongoing journey, not a one-time event?

5. What's your next step in walking boldly into the life God has for you?

Epilogue

What does it feel like to stand in a garden awash with sunlight, every petal open in radiant color? In your hands, you hold the journey from hidden hurt to flourishing life: *Scarred* taught you to name your pain, *Mended* showed you the habits of restoration, and *Bloom* invited you to step into a wholeness that defies the old confines of trauma. Now, here you are, at the close of these pages, having watched seeds of resilience emerge from the once-barren soil of heartbreak. The question now is not whether you can bloom but how far your bloom will stretch.

When you first began, you might have felt unsure that light could find its way into those darkest corners of your experience. Yet each chapter coaxed you to trust that a sprout does push through the heavy ground, that healing isn't merely a general idea but an unfolding truth in your everyday life. The overshadowing gloom once told you that your story ended where your wounds began—but you've since discovered a truth stronger than your pain: your life was destined for renewal all along.

In *Scarred*, you turned on the lights in corridors you previously kept locked and dark. You identified the ache you carried and realized you weren't alone in feeling broken or bruised. You took the first step through raw honesty—allowing the air of acknowledgment to ventilate old wounds. That was no small act of courage. It opened the door to everything that followed.

Then, in *Mended*, you forged a daily path toward real, measurable relief. You practiced grounding techniques, set healthy boundaries, dared to speak your truth, and watched as the grip of trauma loosened. The routines and faith-based exercises weren't just tasks on a list; they were your lifeline, guiding you from raw pain to a rhythm of steady restoration. Each habit—morning prayers, evening wind-downs, boundary-setting—became an anchor that steadied your soul in ways you'd never known before.

Finally, in *Bloom*, you discovered that healing is not the end of your story but the beginning of a future bursting with possibility. You ventured into the realm of cultivating joy, stepping into new opportunities, and becoming a source of encouragement. Where trauma once screamed, *"You're finished!"* you rose to say, *"I'm only beginning."* You learned that the scars you carried could become testimonies, each line telling a story of hurt, survival, resilience, and determined hope.

And now you stand here, perhaps feeling excitement and uncertainty at the culmination of these pages. *What does it mean to truly bloom day after day?* It means you continue forward with an openness to God's unfolding plan, even when life's terrain turns rocky or a fresh storm brews.

You remain anchored in the knowledge that your healing journey was never about merely escaping pain but forging a richer, deeper existence where hope stands unshaken despite the winds of adversity.

You might still face triggers or encounter moments when echoes of the past resurface. Remember, blooming isn't about denying the scars. It's about acknowledging how you've changed, how each heartbreak was met by faith that soared beyond despair. Look for the blossoms in the daily hustle—rising for work, caring for loved ones, weaving faith into mundane tasks. They'll appear in sudden laughter you didn't think you could muster, the calm you feel in situations that once triggered panic or the heartfelt ways you find yourself listening to another person's sorrow. These are the signs that your blossoming spirit permeates your everyday reality.

Take heart that you do not journey alone. Whether you've found a supportive friend, a faith community, or an online space of shared stories, these companions serve as your safety net and your cheering squad. Lean on them. And in turn, offer your story as a gift: let your testimony embolden someone else who's still in the shadows, unsure if they, too, can break free. The grace that carried you forward can also carry them, and you become a living parable of hope—a testament that ashes can indeed become beauty.

Consider the final message that resonates through each step of this series: your life is precious beyond measure, shaped by storms but not defined by them, redeemed by a love that never left your side. Where you once asked, "Will I survive?" you can now ask, "How will I thrive in each new day?" Let your answer reflect the fullness that's taken root in your heart. Keep praying, keep dreaming, keep serving, and keep growing. The soil that once felt like a grave of disappointments can be the ground from which your faith blossoms in perpetual color.

In many ways, this is the end of a chapter but not the conclusion of your story. Healing continues in layers. You'll keep discovering hidden strengths, calling forth deeper levels of compassion, forging new paths you never expected. Each fresh season might call you to reevaluate, shift your focus, or expand your circle of impact. That's the rhythm of blooming—never static, constantly evolving.

So, as you close these pages, do so with a sense of accomplishment and expectancy. Accomplishment because you dared to face the scars, build healthy routines, and let your soul bud and flower in faith. Expectancy because tomorrow's horizon promises further rooms of discovery, further vistas of purpose. You walk forward as a living witness to the unstoppable grace that transforms pain into promise.

Thank you for taking *Scarred, Mended, and Bloom* to heart. Thank you for showing up for yourself day by day. And thank you for trusting that, in God's hands, a ravaged field can become a thriving garden. May the lessons and reflections linger in your spirit, guiding your steps as you continue to bloom—petal by petal, day by day, breath by breath—into the fullness of all you're meant to be.

Step forward boldly into life's next chapter, dear soul. The world needs your bloom now more than ever. Keep shining, growing, and believing that the dawn of new beauty is always at hand. Each day you lean into the love that undergirds your journey, your life will reflect a radiant truth: God can raise an abundant, flourishing field of hope from once-scarred soil.

What's Next

Here you are, at the last pages of *Bloom*, having journeyed through a trilogy that began in the darkness of old hurts and ended in the promise of ongoing flourishing. Take a moment to soak in the reality: you confronted the painful echoes of your past (*Scarred*), you actively cultivated habits that brought daily relief and growth (*Mended*), and you have now stepped into a life that beckons with new joy and purpose (*Bloom*).

Yet if there's one lesson repeated across these books, it's that healing doesn't freeze-frame at a final milestone. Instead, it evolves continually, each new season unveiling fresh facets of your resilience and God's grace. *Bloom* has shown you how to flourish, but the garden of your life still holds room for more blossoms. You can keep discovering new ways to serve, new dreams to chase, and deeper layers of empathy for those who still wander in the shadows you once inhabited.

So, *what next?* Embrace the rhythm of daily living that merges your scars and your aspirations. Keep practicing the prayerful routines that center your spirit, lean into communities that uplift you, and keep an open heart for the Holy Spirit's gentle guidance. You might sense a call to mentor others, transform your professional landscape with a new mindset, or radiate kindness in everyday interactions. Each step forward stands on the foundation you laid in these pages—evidence that the toxins of trauma have lost their hold.

If you ever feel a flicker of your old anxieties creeping back, revisit the principles in *Scarred* and *Mended*: re-ground yourself, reaffirm your worth, and remind your soul of how far you've come. Also, rest assured that the God who led you through these chapters hasn't left. The same tender presence that carried you through heartbreak is walking alongside you as you build a future shaped by faith and unburdened by fear.

And if your spirit feels stirred to share your testimony, do so boldly yet compassionately. Countless people remain locked behind the same walls of silence you once knew. Your story—raw and real—can be the key that helps them see that healing is possible and that the wilderness can give way to a blooming field. Each time you share, you strengthen them and yourself, reaffirming that your scars are signposts of grace, not reminders of defeat.

In reading *Bloom*, you've confirmed that your life is not primarily about the trauma you endured but the wholeness you've embraced. Continue living in that wholeness. Continue discovering the extent of your growth because every new day holds opportunities to love more deeply, dream more expansively, and serve more compassionately. May your footsteps carry you with the confidence of one who knows that even the darkest seasons can yield the brightest blossoms. Keep blooming, dear soul. Keep blooming and never stop.

THE END